Unburnable Ambition

Also by Sheekha S.

The IT Girl: 3 Steps to Find Career Options for Young Women in Tech

Unburnable Ambition

How Overachievers Win Without Burning Out

Sheekha S.

Unburnable Ambition © Copyright 2026 Sheekha Singh

ISBN: 978-1-7775463-5-9 (eBook)
ISBN: 978-1-7775463-3-5 (Paperback)

All rights reserved. No part of this publication may be reproduced, distributed, or transmitted in any form or by any means, including photocopying, recording, or other electronic or mechanical methods, without the prior written permission of the publisher, except in the case of brief quotations embodied in critical reviews and certain other noncommercial uses permitted by copyright law.

Disclaimer

Although the author and publisher have made every effort to ensure that the information in this book was correct at press time, the author and publisher do not assume and hereby disclaim any liability to any party for any loss, damage, or disruption caused by errors or omissions, whether such errors or omissions result from negligence, accident, or any other cause.

Adherence to all applicable laws and regulations, including international, federal, state, and local governing professional licensing, business practices, advertising, and all other aspects of doing business in the US, Canada, or any other jurisdiction, is the sole responsibility of the reader and consumer.

Neither the author nor the publisher assumes any responsibility or liability whatsoever on behalf of the consumer or reader of this material. Any perceived slight of any individual or organization is purely unintentional.

The resources in this book are provided for informational purposes only and should not be used to replace the specialized training and professional judgment of a health-care or mental health-care professional.

Neither the author nor the publisher can be held responsible for the use of the information provided within this book. Please always consult a trained professional before making any decisions regarding treatment of yourself or others.

For more information, email riseandtellwithsheekha@gmail.com.

To those who always ask me when my next book is coming out. Here it is!

&

To Onyx, and to the dog-dad who made it impossible for me to write this at home.

Praise for
Unburnable Ambition

"In *Unburnable Ambition*, Sheekha reminds us that we don't have to torch ourselves to shine. With humor and humanity, she flips the myth of burnout on its head—proving that true success doesn't come from running hotter but from burning steadier. It's psychological oxygen for anyone tired of the hustle inferno. This isn't self-help—it's self-combustion for the soul."

—Jodi Wellman, MAPP, author of *You Only Die Once: How to Make It to the End with No Regrets*

"Behind every success lies the often unspoken toll of pushing oneself too hard, risking burnout without realizing it. This inspiring book serves as a balm for that very challenge—a guide for leaders on when to pause, reflect, and re-energize. An essential read for leaders who aspire to lead by example and prioritize sustainable success."

—Anup Cheruvathoor, founder & CTO of Qubo

"In *Unburnable Ambition*, Sheekha brilliantly exposes how the drive for freedom or success can easily turn into self-imposed captivity. Entrepreneurs and professionals alike fall into the trap of overworking, believing nonstop effort equals faster results—only to end up drained. Through sharp insights and real stories, Sheekha shows that true ambition is sustainable when work and self-care coexist. Her message is a powerful reminder that fulfillment isn't found in the hustle but in the harmony between doing and being."

—Regina Huber, transformational leadership coach, inspirational speaker, and author of *Living My Freakin' Amazing Life: Create the Life That's Perfect for YOU – Anywhere in the World*

"Sheekha reminds us that the most powerful story we can tell is our own. This book is a truthful, exciting, and inspiring adventure, so grab a pen, hold on tight, and start creating your next chapter! Because 'when' is always NOW!"

—Capella Fahoome, MSOD, MAPP, PCC, Hollywood producer, organizational leadership coach, and assistant instructor at the University of Pennsylvania

Table of Contents

Praise for *Unburnable Ambition* ix

Foreword xv

Introduction... 1

PART 1 7

    Chapter 1: The Myth of Having It All 9

    Chapter 2: The Lie You Were Raised On 19

    Chapter 3: Productivity P*rn........................... 29

    Chapter 4: When Purpose Becomes Pressure 35

PART 2 43

    Chapter 5: The Courage to Say NO 45

    Chapter 6: The Cultural Weight We Carry . 55

PART 3 63

    Chapter 7: Rest Is Not Laziness 65

    Chapter 8: Money, Fear, and Burnout.......... 73

    Chapter 9: Finding Your True North 81

Chapter 10: Micro-Shifts That Change Everything 89

Chapter 11: Stop Demonizing Your 9–5 95

Chapter 12: Community and Connection . 101

Chapter 13: Designing Your Burnout-Proof Future 107

Chapter 14: Rising and Telling Your Story 117

Afterword 125

Acknowledgments 127

About the Author 129

Connect With Me 131

Foreword

—Timothy Mitrovich, CEO of Artisan Studios

About ten years ago, I was super burned out. I wasn't happy with my job. I felt like I could do more and be more, but I also felt like I was constantly running into the same brick wall.

Everything came to a head during my 2015 annual physical. My doctor reported that my blood pressure was high (135/90) and that I needed to make some immediate changes in my life. The alternative, of course, was to start taking blood pressure medication, but to me that felt like sweeping the core issues under the rug.

Sheekha S.

I started thinking about my stress levels, which invariably led me to analyze my overall happiness and the life choices I was making. I had an infant daughter, and I couldn't help but think about how my life choices would impact her if my health were to decline because I was too afraid to make a change.

My own father had two heart attacks when I was young. He hated his job and felt boxed into his career. He never felt like he could make a change AND support his family, so he stuck with it, in spite of the things that made him miserable every day at the office.

I realized I was doing precisely the same thing. I didn't like my job. It made me miserable, but I stuck with it because I was afraid to make a change. I was afraid of failing.

The more I thought about it, the more I realized something very important: I didn't like many of the people I worked with. I didn't hate them. I didn't even dislike them. But I didn't LIKE them that much either. Yet those were the people I spent over fifty hours with every week. That wears you down. Now add all the other stresses of a job (any job), and you have…high blood pressure.

So I quit my job.

Unburnable Ambition

I decided I'd be a better father and husband if I was happy every day at work. If that meant making less money, then so be it. It took me a few entrepreneurial attempts to find my stride, but eventually I found it with Artisan Studios. I finally had what I was looking for: doing interesting work with people I really, really liked.

I work harder at Artisan and have more responsibility now than I ever did before, but because I work in a healthy environment with people I really like, my blood pressure is back down to 115/70—without medication.

My big takeaway is that you can be ambitious, you can find success, and you can do that while avoiding burnout. But you have to

- like your environment,
- like the people you work with, and
- be unafraid of failure.

To make a long story short:

You spend the majority of your waking hours at work, so it's critical that you work in a healthy environment with people you REALLY like. If your environment isn't healthy and/or you don't REALLY like the people you work with, then it's time to go.

Sheekha S.

The problem is that "going" is scary. It's unknown. You might "fail." The fear of failure and of the unknown causes people to stagnate in places where they shouldn't be—and then they burn out.

Somewhere on the journey from infancy to adulthood, failure becomes unacceptable. Knowing this, and overcoming it, is one of the great "unlocks" in life. If you want to avoid burnout, give yourself the space and the grace to try new things (and fail). In doing so, you'll give yourself the opportunity to get to somewhere new. No one else is going to do it for you.

I love the theme of this book. The pursuit of ambition can rob you of joy and authenticity, but it doesn't have to. Hopefully you can take some of the wisdom found in this book and discover that change is good, failure is not bad, and you can achieve your ambitions without losing yourself in the process. It is never too late to make a change.

Introduction

I Knew Something Had to Break (And It Wasn't Going to Be Me)

I knew something was wrong when I ended up yelling at my dog, my partner, and my mom all in the same day. I saw rainbows in my eyes. You know what I'm talking about—those colorful speckles you see around your eyes. I am glad I didn't cry (not that there's anything wrong in crying), but I knew I had to change. I drank beer like any other overworked, somewhat responsible millennial that just wanted to take the edge off a bad mindset would that night.

Sheekha S.

The next morning, my calendar was full. I had three podcast interviews, my 9–5 job calls, deadlines, uploads, emails, and those damn Slack dings. My hands were shaking.

I had a meeting in five minutes. I tightened my ponytail and put back on the wonderful smile that many have complimented me on. The only difference was it was FAKE this time.

If you've ever hidden your rock bottom under a blazer, a pat, some lipstick, or a smile, you already know what this book is about.

If Mel Robbins and Glennon Doyle had a younger brown immigrant cousin who refused to sugarcoat the truth, that's me.

I was raised to be unbreakable. I grew up with a single mom and my grandmother. I was supposed to make everyone proud. To make my bosses proud. To make myself proud. To be the "Good Indian Girl" who doesn't talk back, the immigrant elder daughter who proves her worth, the corporate professional who keeps going no matter what.

My COO once told me I'm a machine. And for a while, I was.

I did *everything right*. Until my body and mind started saying *no* in every language possible: exhaustion, stress, brain fog, and lack of interest. My ambition was still roaring, but I was crumbling.

I knew being an overachiever came with costs, but I never anticipated I would have to pay so soon.

Here's what I know now.

Burnout doesn't just steal your energy. It steals YOU from your authentic *self*. Most of us keep giving, producing, and performing, hoping someone will notice and hand us permission to rest.

Guess what!

Nobody's coming. Nobody!

You have to give yourself that permission.

When I went looking for answers, I found two things:

1. Endless advice from people who had never worked in the worlds I came from with no clue about the weight of cultural expectations.

2. Inspirational fluff that made me feel like I was the problem because I wasn't meditating enough or thinking positively.

What I didn't find was a voice like mine—someone who understood what it's like to be caught between *two worlds*:

- A culture that teaches you to endure
- A society that wants you to hustle

That's why this book exists, and that's why you're reading it.

This book is for every burnout-prone dreamer who's tired of performing strength.

I'm not here to hand you a "perfect" life plan. I'm here to give you the tools, stories, and truth that I wish someone had given me to help you burn brighter *without burning out*.

Because you don't need to be fixed.

You just need to come back to yourself. The version that is truly YOU.

My Promise to the Reader: By the time you finish, you'll have a new definition of success, a clear picture of who you are without the masks, and the courage to rise and tell your truth without apology.

This is not soft healing. It's a rebellion.

I want you to realize that you aren't broken; you're overprogrammed. If you're a visual learner like me, imagine a laptop that's whirring because it's too hot.

This is NOT a self-help book. This isn't just about self-care. It's about reclaiming your fire, rewriting your story, and refusing to shrink in the face of expectations.

Throughout this book, I've included excerpts and summaries from podcast guests that I've interviewed. I am by no means an expert, but I am someone who has lived through the web of expectations, overachievement, the constant need to prove as someone who wanted it all. I've been there and done that. I'm taking what I learned from others and presenting it to you in this book as a hard-truth, no-fluff package. Real stories from real people. This is how I turned my burnout into a brand and how I've not just lived it but am practicing it.

I believe that a story doesn't have to be PERFECT. It just has to be REAL.

—Sheekha S.

PART 1

Chapter 1

The Myth of Having It All

We were sold a version of success that's killing us.

Once upon a time in 2015, I had a dream job. I had everything I wanted. I was close to getting a master's degree. I was an intern at a Fortune 500 company. I was working full time and attending evening classes three times a week from five to eight o'clock. My husband (boyfriend at the time) and I drove a 2001 Dodge Stratus (yes, a stick). The Americans went crazy whenever I told them I took my driving exam in 2015 with a stick.

Sheekha S.

To be honest, sticks are pretty common in India, and I grew up driving one. It wasn't new to me, so I aced the test. The examiner was impressed too. You should've seen her face when I took her to my car and turned the ignition on.

That was the first time in my life I had actually experienced burnout for real, but unfortunately, the term burnout wasn't trending back then. As an immigrant student, you had to complete your master's, get a job, pay off your loans, and be happy. I was doing all of that, but the truth was I was miserable.

I was a top-notch student who excelled at all my presentations, papers, and assignments, but I hated it. It was eating me up. I hated my internship because I was supposed to wear formal wear even on Fridays. (It's funny how now that I have a completely remote job, I look forward to wearing my $300 Aritzia pants once a year for client visits.)

Success meant having a master's degree (even though it sucked the life out of you), having a full-time job (because you had to maintain your visa), and being able to send some extra money to your family. Going back home was NEVER an option back then. Times have changed now, but expectations haven't.

The Confidence Trap

Us immigrant creatives, high-achievers, dreamers, and doers struggle with one thing that works both *for* us and *against* us.

CONFIDENCE.

Some days we're so confident that we think we can change the world, but on other days, our confidence is our biggest hurdle. We've already painted a picture of ourselves for the world—BOLD, CONFIDENT, OUT THERE, SMART—but when we don't keep up with that image, we consider ourselves failures.

I have realized that burnout isn't a you or a me problem. It's the way expectations are set and the way we do everything to please that system and definition of success.

A 2017 review by Alegría et al. shows how immigrants face higher risks of depression and anxiety, not only due to financial stress but because of cultural pressures and identity conflicts.[1]

Research on fame and success by Mann and Rich found that what society glorifies as "achievement" is often a loop built on

---

[1] Margarita Alegría et al., "Immigration and Mental Health," *Current Epidemiology Report* 4, no. 2 (2017): 145–155.

determination, risk-taking, and the desire for recognition. They identified traits like focus and business skill as predictors of fame but not necessarily of fulfillment. In other words, the very traits that help people climb the ladder can also keep them trapped in it, constantly performing success to prove it's real.[2]

I once had a friend of a friend who didn't have a job or a house and was into drugs, but he always wanted to show off that he was doing great. So he ended up getting not just one but two expensive cars, a dog he couldn't take care of, a boat, a motorcycle, an expensive watch, and a house in the middle of nowhere—all of which ended up raising his expenses. He thought he was successful. He wanted to believe the LIE that all of us are fed—the lie that traps even the best of the best.

SUCCESS = FAME = MONEY = STATUS

We call actors, singers, and businessmen successful. Why?

Because they have money, fame and status. They drive expensive cars, wear expensive shit, and get a pass for whatever unintellectual garbage they spew out, and we all CRAVE that.

---

[2] Monroe Mann and Jonathan Rich, "Developing a Measure to Predict Fame and Success," *Psychology Research* 10, no. 6 (2020): 213–230.

Unburnable Ambition

We want what they have, but if you ask me, on a deeper level, they're not successful at all.

I'd ask them to define success and to define freedom.

This isn't just my experience. A 2016 study by Yucesoy and Barabási supports this disconnect between real achievement and perceived success.[3] They found that while exceptional performers in tennis like Federer or Djokovic earned fame through measurable excellence, many others gained popularity for reasons completely detached from performance. In other words, success today isn't just about skill or substance; it's about visibility. The same is true outside of sports. We've built a culture that rewards those who look successful rather than those who truly are.

This proves that the myth of "having it all" isn't just about immigrants or cultural expectations. It's universal. No matter your background, success defined through someone else's lens will burn you out.

Success is a drug that works against you if you don't have control over your life. It's a lie that was fed to us when we were kids.

---

[3] Burcu Yucesoy and Albert-László Barabási, "Untangling Performance from Success," *EPJ Data Science* 5, no. 17 (2016).

Sheekha S.

Go to college, get good grades, get a job, buy a house, get a car, marry a good person, get promoted, travel, save for retirement.

OK, I did all that. Now what?

What next?

I hate to think this is what it was all about. I hate the idea that people tie success to being able to survive and pay bills when life is so much more than that.

This is predominant in immigrant culture, but the more I spoke with kids and parents in the Western world, the more I understood that the same lie was being fed everywhere else too.

Hard work is always glorified.

I'm not alone in saying this. Research in the Canadian Medical Association Journal highlights how acculturative stress and discrimination can worsen the risk of burnout among immigrants, echoing the cultural weight I described earlier.[4]

---

[4] Laurence Kirmeyer et al., "Common Mental Health Problems in Immigrants and Refugees: General Approach in Primary Care," *Canadian Medical Association Journal* 183, no. 12 (2011): 959–67.

The Glorification of Hard Work

Tell me the first thing that comes to your mind when you think of a farmer (this is true in all cultures).

HARD WORK

They wake up at the crack of dawn and work "hard" all day, only to get the profits after two quarters. That's half a year. That is a LOT of work, but the same concept is applied to all other domains.

Working late means you're working hard. Working on the weekends means you're a star employee. Dude! No! In my opinion, if you are working after-hours or need extra time to do your job, that means one of two things:

1. You are not productive in the time that has been allotted to you, OR
2. You suck at communicating estimates for the task that you're working on.

Working hard doesn't mean you're producing quality work, and hard work doesn't automatically equate to success by any means.

I want you to understand that the game is rigged. If you are someone who ends up putting in more effort and more hours even though you aren't getting paid for it, then it's high time you realize that your employer is using you and that you're never getting promoted.

Learn the game. Play it. Get better.

That's how you win.

The Next Big Thing

Meta-analytic evidence shows that even "high-functioning" professionals see their daily performance erode under chronic burnout.[5]

Everything is designed to make you spend more, earn less, and pay more taxes, but where's success in the grand scheme of things?

Remember how your teachers and peers used to say, "Ah, you are definitely going to do something someday. You are going to be the next big thing"?

Well, what happened?

Did you make it?

Do you call a thousand unfinished projects "doing something big"?

---

[5] Arnold Bakker et al., "Burnout and Work Engagement: The JD-R Approach," *Annual Review of Organizational Psychology and Organization Behavior* 1 (2014): 389–411.

If you are exceptionally talented but are still stuck paying your mortgage, credit card debts, and loans; doing your job with no time to do what you love; and struggling to see the light at the end of the expectations tunnel, how can you say you've "made it"?

You are just like any other person who is managing to survive in this world. I had the best job and a degree, but it drained me. I was hired as a software engineer, but I chose not to be a developer. I pivoted to breaking the code instead of making it. That was the first step I took because I wanted to love my job. I didn't want to fail.

Tools to Remember the Important of Thoughts:

- **Reflection exercise**: Write down the version of success you grew up believing versus the version you secretly crave.

- **Myth checklist**: Notice the signs that you've bought into the lie (e.g., you work late to prove your worth, you measure yourself by status symbols, you feel guilty for resting).

It starts with you and what you think. If you are constantly stressed out, your thoughts will be stressed, and you'll have no energy left to recognize your own strengths. Stop thinking that you are failing. Instead, understand how things really work.

Stop smiling while you're sinking.

But how do you even know when you're sinking? That's where we'll go next.

Chapter 2

The Lie You Were Raised On

I have always been a results-oriented person. I like proof and I love transformations. I'm overly obsessed with self-growth and self-improvement topics, hence my podcast, *Rise & Tell with Sheekha*. If I've learned one thing from all the guests I've interviewed so far, it's the importance of doing what you said you would do without excuses.

Burnout is no different. When you end up taking on too much like I did, you generate negative emotions because you want to do more. You love it, but it's killing you from inside. The problem here is that you don't even realize you're experiencing burnout because you were always taught to excel at your work, be perfect all the time, and never stop hustling.

High-functioning people and ambitious people don't realize the stress until it is too late. As Sudipto Roy argues, systemic stress is no longer just an individual problem. It is baked into how modern society rewards ambition and inequity.[6]

Here's a rundown of everything I had on my plate:

- Hosting a podcast
- Growing three YouTube channels
- Writing a book
- Working a full-time job
- Running a household
- Maintaining friendships and relationships
- Traveling
- Managing finances
- Making time for fitness
- Building a brand
- Leading a business

---

[6] Sudipto Roy, "Ambition, Inequity and Systemic Stress: Causes and Consequences in Modern Society," *Social Science Journal for Advanced Research* 5, no. 3 (2025): 105–111.

- Attending conferences and virtual talks/keynotes

Why?

Blame the lies that were fed to me.

Be grateful, work hard, and don't want too much—all the cultural, gender-based immigrant values we internalize. I had an identity conflict. Like, who even am I without all this?

Who am I if I'm not a high achiever? At school, I used to be at the top of my class, involved in sports, debates, drama, events, clubs, everything. You name it, I did it.

So when I realized I was burned out, I had some very hard questions to answer.

Indicators of Burnout

A 2006 study published in the Journal of Continuing Education in Nursing describes the indicators of burnout as feeling:[7]

- Overworked,
- Emotionally drained,
- Frustrated, and

---

[7] Karen E. Espeland, "Overcoming Burnout: How to Revitalize Your Career," *Journal of Continuing Education in Nursing* 37, no. 4 (2006): 178–84.

- Less productive.

Many people also notice these additional symptoms:

- Feeling disconnected
- Constantly reinventing yourself

You don't need a quiz or a survey to find out if you're experiencing burnout. This short list is enough for you to recognize what you are currently feeling.

Who Are You?

I went to Nicaragua once on a yoga retreat in San Juan del Sur. The view from the shala was breathtaking. The instructor made us sit in a circle so everyone could introduce themselves (specifically where we worked and what we did) before we spread out our mats for the actual session.

The sun was setting, and it was supposed to be a yoga nidra class. As my body started to relax, the teacher asked us all to close our eyes and think about who we are without our labels. She said, "For the next few minutes, take a deep breath and ask yourself how you can introduce yourself without labels. Who are you without your job, your salary, and your status? What are you?"

Unburnable Ambition

That hit me hard.

As an immigrant and highly ambitious person, I always related success to labels.

The 2006 study I just referenced also mentioned that in order to revitalize a career and move away from burnout, you need to change your thought processes and viewpoints about the people and things that may be contributing to your burnout.[8]

For me, it started with facing the lie I was living and figuring out what actually gave me joy.

There are always going to be signs. Signs that scream you are not okay even if it looks like you're killing it. Your body is warning you, and you need to normalize noticing these signals and prioritizing yourself.

It is NOT okay to dismiss your energy levels, high cortisol levels, and emotional state. Stop fueling your burnout by increasing your work and overdoing things because someone said you were killing it. Use those compliments to boost your ego, not to strain yourself even more trying to be someone you're not.

Michael Dillard told me on an episode of *Rise & Tell* that during his time as a regional financial controller in South Africa, he was handling

---

[8] Espeland, "Overcoming Burnout," 178–84.

million-dollar projects and supporting over four hundred staff members.[9] He admitted he was always working, and eventually he burned out.

What changed everything for him was having a coach. It reset how he led, gave him his time back, and allowed him to log off at 5:00 p.m., relax on weekends, and actually show up better. His story is proof that burnout doesn't just come from working hard. It comes from working without systems or support.

Nobody has got it all. Nobody can have it all. You need to ask yourself if this is worth it. Hustle culture gets a bad rap, but I realized that it comes at a cost. Your relationships are affected. Your health starts to deteriorate. Why? Because you were trying to show off that you can handle everything and that you've got this.

The truth is you don't.

There, I said it.

Signs You Are Not Okay

Here are some of the warning signs that you're not okay:

---

[9] Michael Dillard, guest, *Rise & Tell with Sheekha*, episode 33, "From Poverty to Financial Freedom | Michael Dillard's LEAD & SAVER Framework for Life & Business," August 13, 2025.

- You're struggling with sleep, digestion, or energy crashes.
- You're overworking without recovery.
- You're hiding your exhaustion.
- You're dealing with unexplained body aches.
- You're snapping at loved ones.
- You're constantly irritable.
- You're becoming more cynical.
- You're numb.
- You're running on fumes without realizing it.

Sound familiar?

One year, when I was trying to do it all, I foolishly allowed guests to schedule podcast interviews with me multiple times a day. I started my day with a podcast interview, reading up on my guest, preparing questions, and setting up the studio. Following that were work calls, my actual 9–5 job, and projects. I'd used my lunch hour to record another podcast interview, then get back to work, before ending the day with two more interviews.

I barely cooked dinner and spent the rest of the night planning YouTube videos, writing books, finding clients for my tech consulting business, revising contracts, updating websites, researching, setting up my Shopify page, editing my show notes, creating video thumbnails, finishing the podcast episodes, scheduling uploads, and editing personal travel vlogs.

Since I was staring at screens nonstop all day and night, I couldn't sleep till 3:00 a.m. One night, I was awake till 5:30 in the morning, and I had to get up at 7:30.

My Garmin watch sends me an alert every day at 9:30 p.m. For half a year, I saw the alert "stressful day" every night. I used to be obsessed with my sleep score and never had anything less than an 80, but now I was in the 50s. As someone who was used to getting all A's, I'm sure you know how hard that was for me.

I soon started to notice my skin was breaking out, and my face was always bloated. Despite the inflammation, I drank a pint of beer at least every day, claiming that I deserved it since I was always busy.

So, if you're in this stage, here's a reminder to notice these red flags early on before it is too late. When you do see them, don't ignore them. Accept it and own it. It's not easy, but once you own it, you will automatically start trying to figure out how not to be burned out all the time.

The Job Demands–Resources model published in the Journal of Applied Psychology explains how output obsession leads to burnout: "When demands outweigh resources, exhaustion is inevitable."[10]

Whenever someone asked me, "What are you trying to point out with this book," I always told them, "There are hundred books on burnout but none that were written by immigrants who have seen both cultures, tried to blend in, and now want to reclaim their life."

I want you to reignite that fire you lost without affecting your body or your mental state. I'm not going to tell you to meditate or try to inspire you. I'm here to give you the straight truth from real stories and experiences from real people that will make you rethink your approach.

I once read a book on visual intelligence that stuck with me for so long. It was embarrassing that although I excelled at finding things others failed to notice, I struggled to notice what was going on inside of me, and I had nobody to blame except my choices.

Tools for Spotting Quiet Burnout:

- Notice your body signals (sleep, digestion, skin, irritability).

---

[10] Evangelia Demerouti et al., "The Job Demands–Resources Model of Burnout," *The Journal of Applied Psychology* 86, no. 3 (2001): 499–512.

- Watch your metrics (fitness trackers, sleep scores, daily schedule).
- Question your labels (introduce yourself without job titles).

I was feeding the system and inherently causing systemic stress, and it was out of control. The pressure was too much.

But if signs aren't enough to wake us up, why do we keep pushing? That's where productivity obsession comes in.

Chapter 3

Productivity P*rn

We are obsessed with output.

There are always people who you think are better than you. I'm a curious soul. I want to know how people do it. I keep asking my guests on the podcast the same thing: "How did you do it?" There were common themes, but the one that was most talked about was productivity.

My Name Is Sheekha, and I Am a Productivity Addict

When I was young, my mother used to tell me and my sister, "Don't study for five hours.

Study for one hour, but do it well and absorb it all." That had a profound impact on me growing up. My friends would ask my mom how much I studied at home because I was always all over the place, participating in a bunch of competitions and organizing events, and yet I was top of my class every single semester. I used to skip classes, hang out with my friends at a coffee shop, and organize activities for clubs, and yet I managed not just to learn what I was taught, but I would explain it to my classmates the day of the exam.

I carried that with me into my adult life and strived to be at the top of my friend circle, the top performer at work, the top-dog mom. I was obsessed with being on top in life that I committed to multiple projects, like the podcast, vlogs, books, and so much more.

The Rise and Fall of a To-Do List Queen

A 2018 study from Kim et al. found that cultural stress and parenting styles significantly shape immigrant children's mental health, showing how early the success-pressure cycle begins.[11]

---

[11] Su Yeong Kim et al., "Culture's Influence on Stressors, Parental Socialization, and Developmental Processes in

Unburnable Ambition

Hustle culture became my identity. I was beaming with pride because I was hustling more than anyone in my circle. I thought I was succeeding because of how obsessed I was with my output. Weekly podcast episodes, weekly vlogs, Instagram posts, short videos, book writing, editing, working as a leader, starting a business, getting client feedback, buying properties, maintaining a clean house.

I was a productivity addict. I was that person who would tell people to do this, do that, do it now, do it this way, etc. I didn't realize who I was anymore without my to-do list. I was always looking for what's next. The high I got from checking items off the list was insane. At one point, I had four separate lists at the same time. I should be given an award for setting up unrealistic expectations for myself. I was filling up pages of notebooks with little square boxes and tick marks.

It cost me my peace, my real joy, and actual rest. It cost me my creativity because I was obsessed with trying to please the target audience through catchy titles and thumbnails. Trying to blend in by creating click-worthy content when I could have spent the same energy creating or drafting my cool dystopian

---

the Mental Health of Children of Immigrants," *Annual Review of Clinical Psychology* 14 (2018): 343–370.

sci-fi romance novel that would make me use my brain and get the creative juices flowing.

On an episode of my podcast, Michael Hopf, cofounder of Beyond the Fray publishing house and a renowned author, told me not to fixate on perfect paragraphs in a rough draft. Get everything on the page first and stay in the flow. Then you can celebrate finishing the draft and start rewrites.[12]

I could relate to this because I know how hard it is to not edit while writing your rough draft. It might be something else for you based on your hobby and skills, but Michael's suggestion applies. When I usually end up fixating on a certain project, I tend to notice that I no longer enjoy it. I obsessed over whether I would be able to check everything off my list by the end of the day. I even designed (and almost published) a to-do list notebook. I'm glad I didn't.

In 2024, Quantum Workplace reported that more than a third of employees now experience high burnout levels.[13] It's proof that

---

[12] Michael Hopf, guest, *Rise & Tell with Sheekha*, episode 36, "Discipline Over Inspiration: Michael Hopf on Writing, Editing & Growth | Rise & Tell Podcast," September 8, 2025.

[13] "Addressing Employee Burnout: 9 Trends Impacting Employee Success," Quantum Workplace, last modified April 3, 2025.

output obsession is everywhere, not just personal.

Stop being obsessed with output!

Things can wait, and the world is not going to end if you don't finish that damn presentation or respond to that email.

As an article from Psychology Today points out, high achievers often mask burnout with performance until the collapse becomes unavoidable.[14]

The truth is I no longer think there can be a "healthy obsession" over anything ever. The word "obsession" itself signifies something intense that can't be healthy. I learned that the hard way.

Tools to Detox from Productivity Obsession:

- One Priority Hour (OPH)
    - Block 60 minutes every day for the single task that actually moves your life/work forward. No notifications. No tabs. No "quick" emails.

---

[14] Marlynn Well, MD, JD, "Why High Achievers Miss the Warning Signs of Burnout," Psychology Today, May 14, 2025.

Sheekha S.

- Create-Before-Consume
    - Spend 30 minutes creating (writing, sketching, outlining) before you open your email, Slack, or social media. Creativity first; reaction later.
- Weekly Output Audit
    - List everything you shipped this week. Circle only the one or two things that truly mattered. Cut one low-value recurring task next week.
- Mentor/Coach Check-in
    - Borrow Hopf's question: "Am I having fun?" If not, change either the goal, the pace, or the support.
- Follow Hopf's rule: Finish the messy draft → Celebrate → Rewrite. No polishing mid-flow.

Chapter 4

When Purpose Becomes Pressure

I had turned my passion into my paycheck, thinking it would protect me from burnout. Instead, the thing I loved most, my work, began to feel like a cage. Every project had to be perfect. Every opportunity had to be taken. I didn't realize I had replaced one form of pressure with another.

Passion is not a shield. It's not a badge of honor if it's eating you up from inside. My passion was not getting me money, but I was already in too deep trying to make it work.

Passion ≠ immunity to burnout

I thought passion would save me. But the experts say otherwise. Research by Vallerand et al. shows that passion can either be harmonious (energizing) or obsessive (draining).[15] The latter often leads to burnout.

I was passionate about passion. You read that right: *was*. I'm starting to despise the term passion. Yes, finding passion is necessary, and I know how important that step is. But for us dreamers, passion is like a slow cancer that doesn't show up on tests at first until one day, boom, you're at stage 4 and it's too late.

I realized very late that it was on me to avoid this pressure. I misunderstood, and I underestimated the timing. I thought finding passion meant the first step to being successful was already done, but that was so far from the truth. I let passion seep into my life to the point where I couldn't figure out the difference between passion, profession, and dreams.

Passion: The Toxic Trait

I loved public speaking. I was fervent about writing. I was passionate about being passionate, and it showed whenever I spoke to

---

[15] Robert J. Vallerand et al., "Les Passions de l'Âme: On Obsessive and Harmonious Passion," *Journal of Personality and Social Psychology* 85, no. 4 (2003): 756–67.

people, when I entered meeting rooms, when I gave presentations, and when I made new connections. Because of that passion, I set a goal for myself to have fifty podcast episodes out by the end of the year.

And guess what? The overachiever in me didn't just publish fifty episodes. I created enough content to last up to seven months if I posted one podcast interview every week. This was insane, but I didn't realize creating goals for myself meant burning myself out like a moth in a flame.

If you want to know why I created this insane goal and why I ended up burning up under the pressure, well, it's because I'm someone who doesn't just listen to advice but actually implements it. No matter who I spoke to—especially the experts in the field, life coaches, and mentors—everybody suggested finding your passion and creating a goal. So I began with a goal of publishing fifty episodes by the end of the year, which meant that I had to research and talk to people every day, and not just record the episodes but also edit them. I found my passion for being a podcast host because I loved talking.

When I met my friends or relatives, I would end up asking them questions about their life and about their struggles, and somehow most of them would compliment me on the way I speak or how good I am at getting answers and information out of people. They said I was talented and suggested I start a podcast. Like any other self-help obsessed person, I too had a to-do list, quarterly goals, and yearly goals.

One of the main goals in my life besides publishing a second book was starting a podcast. One day, I opened a notebook and started listing twenty-five topics that I knew about at that time and felt comfortable talking solo about for at least twenty minutes. Fast forward a year later, and I had no idea that this wonderful dream of mine to become a podcast host would be one of the reasons I burned out.

Toxic Positivity

Looking back, it was ironic. My first episode was on toxic positivity, and that was exactly what was happening to me in real life.

Toxic optimism tells us that we love our work, and because of that, we must endure everything it puts us through. It needs attention, and it craves importance. It's highly demanding. I'd keep telling myself, *Oh, it's going to be worth it one day*, but in reality, it wasn't serving my purpose. I was pressured by my passion, and I started to become a slave.

As psychologists define it, toxic positivity is the belief that no matter how bad things are, you should maintain a positive mindset—even at the cost of your own truth.

I had no boundaries. I would take on guests anytime I was free, regardless of whether I had plans. I would skip events because I had a podcast interview scheduled.

I was constantly exhausted because my work was performance driven.

My perspective changed when I realized that my purpose was never to be an exhausted, drained, and mean bitch.

I spoke with Ambreen Khan, author of *Love Squared*, on my podcast, and she said,

> A lot of us ambitious girls tend to be ambitious because we felt like we had to compensate for our presence. We had to be something for us to be accepted. But, oh my god, girl, you're enough. You're enough. You're beautiful. You are capable. You're confident. You're intelligent just as you are right now.[16]

You don't need a mile-long to-do list to prove your value.

---

[16] Ambreen Khan, guest, *Rise & Tell with Sheekha*, episode 30, "Tech Professional & Author Ambreen Khan on Writing What Others Won't," July 23, 2025, 47 min., 16 sec.

Since actions speak louder than words, I want you to go through this exercise right now. It's not going to take long. You can do this while going on a walk, while you're scrolling on your phone before bed, or even if you're on a flight reading this book. Pay attention, because I want you to remember this one thing.

It's okay to love something and still need to step back.

Tools to Get You Back on Track:

- **Passion:** Ask yourself, "Is this still lighting me up or just keeping me busy?"
- **Pressure:** Set a "stop" time for passion projects.
- **Reset:** Determine if your sense of value is tied to what you produce or how you live.

Once you've done this exercise, reframe your mindset. Remember to stop glorifying being busy.

The Art of Knowing When to Stop

I was busy producing weekly content, but when I took these three simple steps, it changed my outlook. Yes, I was busy, but was creating weekly content still lighting me up? The answer was no. I loved podcasting, and I loved talking to different people each week, and I loved knowing their stories because storytelling is my favorite thing in the universe. How could someone like me who was obsessed with meeting new people and learning new stories become tired and exhausted with those same things?

Once I realized that I needed to change my schedule, I decided to set a stop time for my passion projects. When you set a goal, it doesn't automatically come with a deadline. You have to set a stop time for yourself. That means your project should have specifics on how many hours will be allotted toward it. Even if you're in the flow, even if you're in the zone, even if you're being hyperproductive, you need to come to a stop, and you have to plan what this stop time looks like for you.

This is why I hated the productivity propaganda and the passion agenda. I always read articles and hear people who say you have to make the most of your mornings or evenings. I ended up being affected by this whole idea of being productive and producing all the time because I would hardly take breaks. I wanted to make the most of the time that I had and the zone that I was in, so I wouldn't stop.

I never had an end time, and that's how I ended up messing up my sleep cycle. Since I was in the zone and I was in the mood, I had bursts of energy here and there. If I was writing my book,

I would either write five thousand words one day or write two words the next day.

It was the same with my podcasts. I would struggle to maintain that level of enthusiasm and energy if I had multiple interviews on the same day. I started to regret not scheduling time for my workout. I hated the fact that I couldn't make the most of summer outside, either walking or running, because I always had something to do on my calendar without a clear stop time.

To me, setting a stop time meant only dedicating ninety minutes for my podcast interviews and one hour for my book. This method helped me produce higher-quality content, and I now understood the importance of adding value to my life and not just doing it for the sake of passion.

If there's one takeaway that I want you to get from this chapter, it's this:

Your value isn't tied to producing. It's tied to living.

PART 2

Chapter 5

The Courage to Say NO

Have you ever made plans you were excited about, then, on the day, dreaded getting up, showered, and dressed? That dread is a sign of burnout. I'd hype up trips, dinners, even big purchases...and when it was time, I wanted to stay in bed.

Here's my real problem: I didn't have the courage to say no. Every yes felt like proof of my worth. But every yes was a no to my energy.

When I asked Scott Maderer, a leadership coach, about burnout and time management, he said,

> The most important word in the English language that those folks learn, it's a really hard word to say.

> It's got two letters. It starts with N, and it ends with O. It's no. Because what happens is usually burnout comes from your saying yes to one of two things: either too many things or the wrong things. Both of those will burn you out. Because again, learning to say no is actually a really hard skill to develop.[17]

Saying no isn't rejection; it's resource management.

In my twenties, I struggled with saying no to my own family and friends whom I had known since we were three years old. It wasn't until my early thirties that I actually stood for myself and learned that it is okay to say no. Whenever someone asks me for my advice or my suggestion, this is one of the top things that I tell everybody both in my professional circle and in my personal circle.

Learning to say no is the biggest gift you can give to yourself.

I said yes to everything. Hosting dinners, ceremonies, last-minute plans, because that's what "good girls" do. Especially as an immigrant daughter, I was taught to mold, smile, and agree. Coming from a certain culture meant compromising and saying yes to anything and everything. The reason I was so drained was because I was expected to behave everywhere,

---

[17] Scott Maderer, guest, *Rise & Tell with Sheekha*, unpublished episode, n.d., 46 min., 23 sec.

Unburnable Ambition

fake it in front of certain people, and agree to certain topics and discussions even if I didn't want to.

I remember one situation so vividly. One day a coworker of mine asked if my husband and I could come over to her house that Friday evening for a casual dinner. She mentioned that she'd been dying to hang out with us and that she'd been waiting for our schedules to free up so she and her husband could spend time with us.

Truth be told, I didn't like that coworker very much, and so I never initiated any plans with her or her husband—until she walked up to me and said, "Hey, here's my address. Why don't you and Simon come to my house at 8:00 p.m. this Friday?" I struggled to say no and caved in.

I learned my biggest lesson that Friday. I assumed that it was just going to be the four of us. We walked in to find a room packed with twenty people and a full spread, and the instant regret hit. I smiled through it, but inside, I couldn't wait to go home.

Simon asked me on the way home if I'd had fun, and I told him I didn't want to be the kind of person who fakes having a great time in front of people. He called me out and said, "You need to change this if you're not okay with it. Nobody is forcing you to fake a smile, and nobody's forcing you to attend parties. You are an adult, and you have the right to say no if you're not interested in doing something. If you hadn't gone, she'd have twenty guests instead of twenty-two. Nothing would change, except you'd be happier."

I was one of those people who would struggle to strike difficult conversations and who would walk away whenever something vulnerable came up. I thought I was being selfish whenever I would consider saying no to events or ceremonies that didn't make sense to me. It wasn't until recently that I realized saying no is not selfish; it's self-respect.

Boundaries Are Self-Respect in Action

Cultural guilt is real and heavy. As an immigrant, boundaries can feel undeserved. They aren't, but it can feel like you're betraying everything that you were taught growing up. I strive to crush this guilt now, and I haven't been happier since I started to say no.

When my husband and I were kids, we would say yes to whatever we were asked to do, even if it went against our values. We did it because we wanted to be there for our friends, and we didn't want any beef with our families. But over the last several years, we started to rightfully say no to things that no longer align to our values because we now realize what drains us and what excites us.

I used to lie to people if I didn't want to meet them or make time for them. I thought I was being nice, and I thought I was doing myself a favor because I wouldn't have to fake a smile or pretend that I was enjoying it.

I no longer lie. I clearly tell people that I don't believe in certain ways of doing things and not to take it personally when I turn down events. I told my friends, "Don't use festivals as the only excuse to meet me. We can hang out even if there is no reason or nothing to celebrate."

When you start standing up for yourself and your beliefs, you realize who your true friends actually are. If your friends really understand you and respect you, they will respect your choices. The ones who are still trapped in cultural guilt will make you feel guilty and horrible for not lying to them or for being too straightforward with your beliefs and choices. This makes recovering from burnout even harder.

Burnout recovery demands ruthless prioritization.

Yes, your friends or your family will likely not understand the first time you set boundaries, and they might argue with you, but rest assured that this will pay off in the long run. They'll turn around. I know you will doubt yourself and will question whether you did the right thing. You're going to think, "What are my friends going to think of me? Will they be okay? Did I disappoint them? Am I a bad friend?" But listen. You cannot make others happy if you aren't happy.

My mother, sister, and some of my friends still struggle to set boundaries with their relatives, co-workers, and friends. When I ask them what the problem is, they give me excuses about community bonds and friendship—to which I tell them the community and the bond that they're talking about isn't real if they aren't being true to themselves. People can feel when we're not being real.

Saying no doesn't just apply to your personal relationships. If you're a working professional, this should be one of your top strengths. Trust me when I say this: Your career will massively improve when you start saying no and setting clear boundaries with your coworkers.

I like delivering quality work. I believe that your work speaks for itself. I was once on a project with an incompetent product owner. I struggled to say no, and he knew how to make my life messier. So what ended up happening was I stepped in and started doing parts of his job.

Unburnable Ambition

It started with reminders and with nudges. I was so frustrated that the work wasn't getting done, and instead of reminding him, I ended up doing most of his work. He got used to it and took public credit for every single thing that I did.

I was on a call with this person, the client's VP, and two other people, and without even a hint of shame, he showed off everything that I did and took credit for it in front of me. Because the client was in the meeting, I couldn't call him out.

I hated myself. My confidence wobbled. I couldn't bear the fact that I was the strong, bold leader of the team and yet I let this person just walk all over me. I felt helpless. That was the day I decided I wasn't going to do this anymore.

The next morning, I chose a different approach—I told my boss I was done doing his role. He was an amazing guy. He said, "Don't apologize, Sheekha. You're just setting boundaries, and I wish you would have done this sooner." That changed me.

The next week, the product owner said, "I need this by Friday. Let's go over it now so it's easier."

I asked, "Is there anything specific you need from me?"

When he listed tasks that were under his role, I said, "Hey, these don't fall under my responsibilities. I'm at capacity. As a Scrum Master, I can support A/B/C. Let me know if you need that."

He paused and said, "Got it. Thanks."

The dynamic changed because I changed and I stood up for myself. I felt almost ecstatic. I was so close to crying (but I didn't, obviously).

As Brené Brown's research highlights, saying no is an act of courage and self-respect, not selfishness.[18]

No Is a Full Sentence

Please, please, please stand up for yourself even if it doesn't come to you naturally. Find the courage to say no. Practice it at home. Try it once a week with events that you don't want to attend, movies you don't want to watch, food you don't want to eat, and things you don't want to do. Then move on to coworkers, then friends, then your family, and be vocal in a way that sits well with everybody.

You don't have to be a bitch about saying no to stuff you don't like. You don't have to be harsh

---

[18] "What I Learned From Brené Brown: How to Set Clear Boundaries," Blue Osa, last modified March 20, 2025.

to be clear. Be kind. Be firm. But muster the courage first to stand up for yourself because you deserve it. At the end of the day, you're going to be so proud of yourself for standing up and for knowing what you're worth.

Okay, so now that we've determined why we need to stand up for ourselves and that we need to learn to say no, here are some of the things that can help you. I started doing this five years ago, and it's made my life a lot better than it used to be.

How do you set a boundary? Use these tools.

The No-Without-Guilt Kit

- **Boundary Script**: "I appreciate the offer, but I can't commit right now."
    - Optional follow-up: "If that changes, I'll reach out."
- **Yes Filter**: Only say yes if it's a hell yes or aligned with your ninety-day goals.
    - Everything else is a no/not now.
- **Delay Default:** "Let me check my capacity and get back to you."
    - This gives you space to choose without panic-agreeing.
- **No Guilt Journal**: Track each no → Note what it created.
    - Time, rest, joy = higher-quality yeses.

- **Work Script (role clarity):** "That task sits with the product owner. My scope is X/Y/Z. I'm happy to support you by doing A/B/C."

Saying no doesn't make you selfish; it makes you truthful. Practice at home. Practice at work. Be clear, be kind, be firm. The people who love you will adjust. The opportunities that are truly yours won't evaporate when you honor your limits. Instead, they'll finally have room to grow, and you'll have room to breathe.

Chapter 6

The Cultural Weight We Carry

When I was growing up in India, I had only two "career options." Either become an engineer or become a doctor. I explain this in detail in my first book, *The IT Girl*.

I told my mom I wanted to be a DJ. Then I told her I wanted to be a journalist. Both dreams were shut down before they had a chance to breathe. My mother, a single parent, then asked me to pick engineering because she couldn't afford medical school. Journalism or music? They weren't even on the table.

It wasn't just me. My friends faced the same pressure. The "safe" path was sold to us as the only path. As an immigrant child, you want to rebel, but you're also aware of the financial distress your choices can cause.

As a child of a single parent, moving abroad was a big step for me and my entire family. With it came invisible baggage, the cultural expectations that can keep us in cycles of sacrifice, overworking, and achievement. And that's how most of us end up working hard and cannot come out of the grind.

Research confirms this. A study published in the International Journal of Intercultural Relations, John Berry explains how the stress of acculturation weighs heavily on immigrants—the constant push and pull between one's heritage and culture, and the host country's expectations.[19]

The Box That Follows Us Abroad

I thought leaving India meant leaving those career boxes behind. I was wrong.

When I met older Indian immigrant parents in the US, I assumed they'd be thrilled their kids

---

[19] John W. Berry, "Acculturation: Living Successfully in Two Cultures," *International Journal of Intercultural Relations* 29, no. 6 (2005): 697–712.

could choose anything from filmmaking to design to entrepreneurship. Doors that didn't exist back home. But no. Despite raising their kids in the most developed country in the world, even abroad, parents still said the same thing: "Doctor or engineer."

It blew my mind. These kids had the privilege of opportunity but the same trap of expectation. The box had followed them across oceans.

It's not that we wanted to just keep paying bills with hefty credit limits and big empty houses. The problem is we were deprived of certain things for so long that now we're scared everything can go away.

The Weight of Inherited Dreams

Dreams get passed down like family heirlooms. "We sacrificed, so you must achieve." It sounds noble. It feels loving. But it can crush anybody.

We don't realize it sooner, but the indirect comments and passive aggression affects children and young adults significantly. I remember relatives telling me and my sister, "Work hard. Your mother struggled so much for you." They meant to encourage us, but what I heard was *You owe us your life.* That weight never leaves. Somehow that constant expectation always lingers in the back of my mind, and so I strive to be the best in whatever I do.

A friend once turned down a promotion to focus on her health and take a gap year. Her parents' response? *We didn't send you abroad for you to rest.* That one sentence carried generations of pressure.

Schwartz et al. published an article in the American Psychologist that highlights how acculturation pressures are tied to identity conflict, which can fuel burnout.[20]

On my podcast, writer, and IT consultant Ambreen Khan shared how she faced this internal tension. She said:

> I went through writer's block in the editing phase. Because I'm like, "Oh my god, what I've written is trash. What is this? What was I thinking?"...I would look at it, and I would get really embarrassed... But then over time, I tried to be more kind to myself. If this was my daughter, for instance, or a beloved friend who had done this, how would I speak to them? Why can't I speak to myself the same way? And then I felt brave enough to come back to it and improve it.[21]

---

[20] Seth J. Schwartz et al., "Rethinking the Concept of Acculturation: Implications for Theory and Research," *American Psychology* 65, no. 4 (2010): 237–51.
[21] Khan, "Tech Professional" 19 min., 35 sec.

Her story proves it. Cultural weight doesn't just shape our careers; it shapes our *inner voice.*

The constant pressure of reminding children that you've sacrificed for them and their future becomes a trap. It causes the children to overwork to the extent that they forget who they are while trying to make your dream come true.

I'm glad that things are changing now with the parents of Gen Z and the next generations. I like parents who don't force their children to choose a career only because they think it's going to pay well. I despise the fact that some immigrant kids are still living their parent's dream and have no clue what they love.

Redefining Success

I have traveled to several countries and have visited many Western cities. I realize that respecting traditions doesn't require living someone else's dream.

Tradition tells us that success equals titles, salaries, and degrees. But what if success was yours to define?

Here's my challenge to you: Write down three success markers that are yours alone.

Here are mine:

- I will be successful when I have no debts.
- I will be successful when I have more friends than emails.
- I will be successful when I can take time off without worrying about PTO, OOO replies, to-do lists, or deadlines.

Now it's your turn. Write down your markers. Pin them where you'll see them. Watch how freeing it feels. You'll be shocked when you actually think about this.

Permission Practice

I want you to compare cultural values with personal well-being. Ask yourself:

- Does this serve me anymore?
- Why am I doing this if it doesn't align with my beliefs?
- If I grew up on the other side of the world, would I still hold on to this, even if it cost me my peace?

Give yourself daily "cultural permission" slips:

- It is okay to rest.
- It is okay to say no.
- It is okay to stop generational traditions that don't serve you.

Yes, it is okay to not let people walk over you.

Unburnable Ambition

It is okay to give yourself permission to stop generational trauma and traditions that do not serve your purpose anymore.

Definitions of success are inherited, but they can be redesigned.

PART 3

Chapter 7

Rest Is Not Laziness

Rest is a productivity multiplier, not a sign of weakness.

I didn't realize my body was begging for rest until I woke up with chest pains. I used to think rest meant weakness. But my body had other plans. I woke up one morning with body aches, random bruises, and exhaustion I couldn't explain. I wasn't training for a marathon. I was just glued to screens—my laptop, phone, camera. I swapped hats all day: podcast host, YouTuber, writer, employee, friend. On paper it looked like all I did was sit at my desk, but in reality, it was draining the life out of me.

Whenever I wanted to rot on the couch with Netflix or doomscroll on TikTok, I'd be hit with the same message, another "Don't waste your evenings" reel making me feel guilty for not hustling harder. I thought I hadn't earned rest.

The meetings, the podcast interviews, the edits, the chapters, the deadlines, the uploads, the business clients, all of it drained me. I was constantly switching and smiling. I was putting myself out there and trying to give 200 percent for everything, but that flame inside me was slowly going out.

True rest is active recovery, not just sleep.

Why It Hit Me So Hard

As immigrants, many of us were raised to equate rest with laziness. Work was worship. Naps were a weakness. The cultural script was *If you're not working, you're falling behind.* That mindset doesn't disappear just because you move to a different country. I carried it into my thirties.

I used to beat myself up for wasting time in front of the TV. So I started creating content and editing from the couch. When I didn't want to use my laptop, I would switch to my phone and edit things there. I was constantly working, and I was constantly producing. My brain didn't have space to let my creativity flow because I had strained my body.

When I interviewed Rapinder Kaur, founder of *Art as Therapy*, she said something that changed me:

> Rest is when you ask when you answer the question, "What do I need?" So you're saying, "You know what? I've had such a day that I cannot do anything other than lie down." That is rest. And I think there's lots of different forms of rest, and you're going to need it at different times, but ultimately the kind of rest that is restorative is always … [when] you pay attention to what's going on in [your body].[22]

That hit me like a punch. I was so busy labeling rest as "wasted time" that I forgot rest could be active recovery.

Research backs this up. In his book, *Why We Sleep*, Matthew Walker shows that deep rest improves memory, creativity, and emotional regulation.[23] A study from Pilcher and Walters found sleep-deprived people perform worse on tasks, even if they "power through."[24]

---

[22] Kaur, "Healing Through Art," 34 min., 40 sec.

[23] Matthew Walker, *Why We Sleep* (Scribner, 2017).

[24] J.J. Pilcher and A.S. Walters, "How Sleep Deprivation Affects Psychological Variables Related to College Students' Cognitive Performance," *Journal of American College Health* 46, no. 3 (1997): 121–6.

Translation: no matter how much coffee you drink, rest outperforms hustle.

Without rest, creativity and resilience collapse.

Some might find certain activities taxing, but for others, they are therapeutic and provide that sense of calmness. Activities that force your body to slow down are needed every day. Rest is not wasting time. In fact, you're doing your body a favor by resting.

After I had done some research on this topic, I started incorporating rest in my daily schedule. Guess what? As sad as it sounds, I scheduled rest for myself. (Yes, I literally added it to my calendar like a podcast recording.)

My Rest Experiments

I cannot afford to take daytime naps, so I began using my lunch hour to intentionally slow down.

- I started fifteen-minute stare breaks. I would go sit in my backyard or front porch without my phone. I scheduled time to stare.
    - Yes, it sounds weird as fuck, but that's what I did. I wish I could show you a screenshot of my calendar slot.
    - I stepped out, sat, or stood for fifteen minutes and just stared at

the trees or my hydrangeas. Laugh all you want, but that helped me!
- The yellow rocking chair routine.
    - I would pour myself a beer, sit in my modern minimalist rocking chair, and call a friend or read a physical book.

My Garmin watch would buzz: "Restful period. Body battery recharged. Stress reduced."

And I'd think, *Hell yes, science agrees*.

I love Garmin, not because I loathe the other brand that dominates the market but because Garmin showed me proof that these experiments were working. I tried what I wanted to recommend in this book for myself, so I can say, yes, it's tried and proven.

So, since we are a more-talk, less-fluff kind of audience, let's get to the meat.

Ten Ways to Recharge Your Body's Batteries

And no Netflix isn't one of them (unless it is followed by "chill" *wink*).

1. **Do nothing:** Block time to stand or to sit without any screens.

2. **Eat light:** Dedicate two days to vegetarian meals. Your body will thank you.

3. **Move outside:** Go on a walk, hike, or run. If you have a dog and they're not reactive, take them with you!

4. **Meditate:** Train your monkey mind for five minutes.

5. **Read a physical book:** No glowing screens allowed.

6. **Choose wisely:** Gather with people who give energy, not drain it.

7. **Dance or exercise:** Both count!

    a. Confession: I can't do more than two pullups. Ugh.

8. **Sleep:** Non-negotiable.

9. **Learn to say NO:** Overcommitment is burnout's favorite fuel.

10. **Travel or take a break:** Break yourself out of your routine and get a change of scenery.

Bonus: Get bored! Boredom is the birthplace of brilliant ideas. Tried and tested.

Rest = ROI

Measure it. Use a watch that can track your sleep, weight, energy, and stress. Watch how "unproductive" rest makes you sharper, calmer, and more creative.

Research shows that lack of sleep impairs creativity, memory, and emotional regulation—exactly what burnout strips away.[25] Intentional recovery activities like unplugging from work and relaxing help restore energy and reduce burnout.[26]

Because here's the truth: Rest is resistance. Rest is saying, *I am not a machine.* Rest is how we reclaim the fire we lost.

---

[25] Walker, *Why We Sleep*
[26] Sabine Sonnentag and Charlotte Fritz, "The Recovery Experience Questionnaire: Development and Validation of a Measure for Assessing Recuperation and Unwinding from Work," *Journal of Occupational Health Psychology* 12, no. 3 (2007): 204–221.

Chapter 8

Money, Fear, and Burnout

I kept saying yes to toxic work because I was scared to lose my paycheck, even when it cost me my health.

Money fears trap us in burnout loops.

When you grow up as an immigrant or child of immigrants, money is never just money. It's survival, stability, and your ticket to belonging.

I still remember when I had $30 in my bank account after paying rent in 2015. I couldn't afford a $50 birthday gift. That moment rewired me. After that, I decided I was never going to be in that position again. That's the immigrant survival mindset.

But here's the catch: Survival mode doesn't turn off. Immigrant survival mindset can override self-care. Even when the paychecks grow, the fear stays. It whispers, *Work harder. Take more projects. Don't say no. You'll lose everything.*

In my opinion, money is a significant contributor to stress.

Research backs this up. Financial stress is one of the strongest predictors of anxiety, depression, and psychological distress.[27] It's not the lack of money alone. It's the fear of not having enough that destroys us.

When Money Steals Rest

Here's the irony: The same money that's supposed to give us freedom often becomes the chain that keeps us hustling.

Vacations? We overdo them. We splurge, then come back broke and stressed. Or we underdo them. We never take them because we're scared to lose paychecks or "look lazy."

---

[27] Soomin Ryu and Lu Fan, "The Relationship Between Financial Worries and Psychological Distress Among U.S. Adults," *Journal of Family and Economic Issues* 44, no. 1 (2022): 16–33.

Neither extreme works. Burnout thrives in extremes.

Take travel as an example. Going on a vacation with my mom feels like I'm reporting for a 9–5 job again but in the mountains or in a different city. While that's taxing to me, it's therapeutic to her. My mom's ideal vacation is cramming in a hundred tourist sites in a week. Mine is sitting on a beach with a book and coconut water. Same trip, totally different ways to recharge. The point? Spending money is only restorative if it aligns with your energy.

Ask yourself:

- Is this an expense that's giving me rest or adding more stress?

- Is this purchase solving today's fear or stealing from tomorrow's peace?

The Fear Trap

Money fears show up in sneaky ways:

- Saying yes to toxic projects because you're scared to lose income.
- Overcommitting to side hustles that drain more than they pay.
- Moving the goalpost (a $1 million goal becomes $5 million, then $10 million, until eventually it's never enough).

Fear convinces us we're one bad decision away from collapse. But here's the truth: Burnout isn't caused by money itself. It's caused by letting fear run the show.

If you can't manage your money, money will manage you. And when money manages you, burnout is guaranteed.

Resetting Your Money/Burnout Cycle

It is true that problems don't last forever, but if you're repeatedly falling into the same financial patterns, then the problem isn't money. It's you.

You can build financial safety without self-destruction.

This isn't a finance manual, but you can't talk about burnout without talking about money.

- Calculate the true cost of overworking.
  - What's your job, side hustle, or "yes" costing you? Time with your kids? Sleep? Health? Joy? Write it down.
- Identify your one-year financial goal.
  - Not ten years, not "someday." One year. It might be to pay off debts, save $5K, fund a vacation, or build a $2K emergency buffer.

- Choose one or two low-burnout revenue streams.
  - Not five side hustles. Not ten projects. Pick the ones that give the best return for the least stress.
- Practice keeping a Fear Journal.
  - Write down every money fear, then counter it with facts.
    - Fear: If I say no to this client, I'll lose my income forever.
    - Fact: I've replaced clients before. One no doesn't end my career.
- Budget for well-being.
  - Instead of saving only for bills or splurges, set a "rest budget." Even $20/month can go toward something that recharges you.

I told you this isn't a self-help book that will guarantee a solution to your problems in one week. All this takes time, and it starts with you figuring out your truth.

I have a question for all my overachievers, to whom this book is dedicated. Have you figured out what success is for you? If you have money, is your money working for you, and can you call yourself successful?

Is money the main reason for your burnout?

Sheekha S.

I'm not someone who is shy of talking about money. I love discussing it. I love learning about it and how it works.

You will never hear me say, "But it's just money. You can earn it again."

If you have bills, mortgage, school fees, family, and monthly subscriptions that put a dent in your paycheck, then you know it is

NEVER

JUST

MONEY.

Unfortunately, that is how our society has been fashioned.

Money is freedom, respect, stability and fear. But if fear keeps dictating your choices, you'll work yourself into the ground and still never feel safe.

- Start learning how to earn more and most importantly how to manage the money you currently earn.
- Start listening to podcasts where people started from scratch and built their wealth (*cough cough* shamelessly plugging in *Rise & Tell with Sheekha*).

Unburnable Ambition

- Ultimately, ask yourself if this is going to unburn you, or if you'll end up being roasted like a chicken leg on BBQ night?

I interviewed the cast and director of the movie *The Science of Getting Rich*, and one of the main themes was to learn and grow.[28] Everyone on my show spoke about changing your mindset around money and working toward growing wealth without excuses. I highly encourage you to check those discussions out.

You don't need a mansion or millions to break the burnout loop. You need clarity: what success costs, what it gives back, and where fear is running the show.

Money should work for you. Not burn you out.

---

[28] *Rise & Tell with Sheekha*, episodes 15–17.

Chapter 9

Finding Your True North

I was following the wrong map. One drawn by other people's expectations.

Harvard Business School professor and author Bill George coined the phrase "discover your true north" in his bestselling book by the same name. He explains how finding your true north is about following your internal compass.[29] Research also shows that meaningful work

---

[29] Bill George and Zach Clayton, *True North* (Jossey-Bass, 2007).

directly predicts life satisfaction and lower burnout.[30]

But here's the catch: It has to be *your* meaning, not someone else's.

I realized I wasn't chasing dreams. I was checking boxes on a map someone else drew for me.

Overachievers always want to do more, to be more. Now that I'm here, I wondered what all this was about. And that's when I found out my truth.

Purpose without clarity is just aimless hustle dressed up as ambition.

For most of my twenties, I was walking on autopilot. Everyone around me was preparing for the GRE, so I thought, maybe I should too. My mom said engineering was safer than medicine, so I did it. People told me to get into IT, get married, get a house, so I did.

But none of those choices came from clarity. They came from the fear of falling behind and cultural pressure to keep up. I wasn't brave enough to take the path less walked on. As immigrants, the map is handed to us before we even know we're allowed to draw our own.

---

[30] Michael Steger et al., "Measuring Meaningful Work: The Work as Meaning Inventory (WAMI)," *Journal of Career Assessment* 20, no. 3 (2012): 322-37.

Unburnable Ambition

Doctor/engineer, safe job, marriage, house. Security comes first. Passion maybe later.

I had a feeling of shame. I questioned my legacy and what I wanted to leave behind. I knew I had to do something, but I had no clarity on what my purpose was. I didn't listen to myself. I decided to walk the road that thousands of others had walked on, and while it looked like success, it wasn't for me. I wasn't being true to myself. Their version of success wasn't sparking joy for me.

In his book *Let Your Life Speak*, Parker Palmer says,

> Before you tell your life what you intend to do with it, listen for what it intends to do with you. Before you tell your life what truths and values you have decided to live up to, let your life tell you what truths you embody, what values you represent...Vocation does not mean a goal that I pursue. It means a calling that I hear.[31]

I wanted to be remembered for something that a typical immigrant family hadn't dreamed of. I wanted to embody my full potential and not hide behind hustle. I wished and craved for something new and different.

---

[31] Parker Palmer, *Let Your Life Speak: Listening for the Voice of Vocation* (Jossey-Bass, 2024), 2–3.

I wanted to be a stout in the world of lagers. Bold. Strong. Different.

That's how you end up burned out while still being "successful."

My Wake-Up Call

I recorded a podcast episode called "Becoming," and it hit me: I wasn't becoming anything I actually wanted to be. I was living out borrowed goals.

When I gave myself permission to pause, things shifted. Writing my book. Recording conversations. Even working on my half-baked sci-fi dystopian novel. These weren't "practical" by traditional standards, but they gave me joy. They recharged me more than any Pilates class or productivity hack ever could.

That's what finding your true north feels like. It's not a perfect plan. It's alignment.

That to me is *becoming*. Becoming the best version of myself that I love. I stopped following the wrong map.

Aimless Hustle vs. True North

Overachievers like us are experts at aimless hustle. We pile on goals without asking if they're even ours.

That's why clarity and not more effort is the best burnout prevention tool.

I was aimlessly hustling. You won't believe the number of startup ideas I pitch to my poor husband every single week. I connect with a lot of overachievers and hustlers on the fact that we all want to do SO MUCH, but we don't know when and how.

Here's what I've heard recently:

- "I know I can start a business, but I don't know if I can do it NOW."
- "I want to be a designer, but I already have three other projects I'm working on."
- "I want to be a photographer, but I don't think it will pay me much."
- "I think I can start a restaurant business, but I am already cooking for my friends and my family."

And then, there's your group of friends that push you to do it because they've seen you succeed in other areas. Your confidence is boosted, and you're now in the middle of ten projects and trying to be the best at every single thing.

Baumeister and Vohs argue that purpose and meaning protect against burnout, but only if they're clearly defined.[32]

Think about it:

- If your energy is spent chasing what others value, it drains you.
- If your energy is spent on what you truly value, it fills you.

If you don't have a purpose in life and the things you do aren't giving you joy, then you're spending your energy on aimless hustle.

Tools to Find Your True North

Your "true north" is a blend of passion, skill, and boundaries.

- **Life Compass:** Pick your top three priorities for the next twelve months.
    - (Here were mine: Fitness, Podcast, Book.)
- **Alignment Test:** Before saying yes, ask yourself, "Does this align with my compass?"

---

[32] R. F. Baumeister and K. D. Vohs, "The Pursuit of Meaningfulness in Life," in *Handbook of Positive Psychology*, eds. C.R. Snyder and S.J. Lopez (Oxford University Press, 2002), 608–618.

- **Focus Filter:** Drop one thing that doesn't align.
    - (For me: attending every social event I was invited to. It didn't fit my compass—or my peace.)
- **Pause Exercise:** Right now, close this book for two minutes. Write down one thing that energizes you when everything else feels heavy. That's a clue to your true north.

Finding your true north doesn't mean you'll never feel lost again. It means you'll always have a compass to come back to. One that points to your values, not someone else's map. It should make you feel worthy and spark joy when you think about your purpose.

So what's your true north going to be?

There's no shame in admitting you were running a marathon on someone else's path and getting burned out when you knew you would kill it with Pilates.

Chapter 10

Micro-Shifts That Change Everything

I used to think burnout recovery meant quitting my job, selling everything, and moving to Bali. Turns out, it started with something way less glamorous. Drinking more water.

Here's the truth: Big change comes from small, consistent actions.

Perfectionism vs. Progress

When we bought our first house in Kitchener, Canada, we dove into DIY projects like any other young homeowner couple. That's when I

Sheekha S.

discovered something about my husband: He's a perfectionist. I, on the other hand, just want to finish, see progress, and keep moving.

Both of us are doers, and we tackle everything with the same zeal and enthusiasm, but one of us can't wait to finish the project and enjoy it while the other can't sleep until it's neat and perfect.

If there's one thing I have learnt, then it's this: when you are in your thirties, there's no guarantee that you're going to have the same energy or excitement on any project as day one. So I believe in getting most done while your body, mind, and energy are on your side.

That reminds me of my background in software engineering. In Agile, you ship the code, bugs and all, then iterate. Perfectionism slows you down. Momentum keeps you alive.

That's true in life too. Perfectionism kills momentum.

There's a reason why the experts recommend just blurting out your thoughts for your rough draft first and don't edit it until later. If you get sucked into editing because you're perfectionist, then that book is never seeing any bookshelf anytime soon.

We favor consistency over perfectionism. Take fitness for example. Nobody walks into the gym and does ten pullups on day one. You suck first. You struggle. Then you improve, rep by rep, shift by shift.

These are the micro-shifts we want to target. Incorporate these micro-shifts that change your lifestyle and help you recover from burnout.

- Stop checking your email the first thing in the morning.
- Stop scrolling through Instagram in the morning.

Mel Robbins says to get up and walk. Stretch. It's not going to be easy, and you will fail, but slowly, these micro changes will become a part of your lifestyle.

The Coffee Swap

For years, I thought I couldn't survive mornings without coffee. It wasn't just caffeine. It was comfort, routine, even small-talk material.

But I knew I wasn't getting enough protein. So I hacked it: oat milk, protein powder, and instant coffee blended together. One week turned into two. Then one Monday, I ran out of coffee. Instead of rushing to buy more, I just skipped it.

And here's the surprise: I felt fine. Better, even. My body didn't crave it anymore. That tiny adjustment became a new ritual.

Micro-shift lesson: You don't need a life overhaul. Swap one habit, stick with it, and let consistency do the compounding.

Why Micro-Shifts Work

Research from 2010 by Lally et al. found it takes about sixty-six days for a habit to become automatic.[33] Not overnight. Not instantly. Just daily reps until it sticks.

That's why so many of my podcast guests—including the cast of *The Science of Getting Rich*—emphasized starting small. Compounding beats intensity every time.

Consistency is the real secret.

If you want to learn more about how small wins compound into transformation, check out Charles Duhigg's book *The Power of Habit*.[34]

---

[33] Phillippa Lally et al., "How Are Habits Formed: Modelling Habit Formation in the Real World," *European Journal of Social Psychology* 40, no. 6 (2010): 998–1009.
[34] Charles Duhigg, *The Power of Habit* (Random House Trade Paperbacks, 2012).

Tools for Micro-Shift Living

Here are some things you could start today.

The 1 Percent Rule: Improve one tiny thing daily.

- Sleep at a set time.
- Wake up at the same time.
- Cut out five minutes of screen time.
- Add one veggie to your meal.
- Clean one room at a time.
- Write twenty words instead of two thousand.

Habit Anchor: Attach new habits to existing routines.

- Stretch right after brushing your teeth.
- Journal right after your morning coffee (or protein shake *wink*).

Weekly Wins: Track small victories to fuel progress.

- Use a journal or apps to track your progress. Seeing your streak can give you an immense boost.

Stop waiting for a "Bali moment." Your comeback starts with water, with one pushup, with saying no to that one extra email.

Sheekha S.

Small doesn't mean insignificant. Small is sustainable. Small becomes automatic. Small is how you unburn yourself.

Chapter 11

Stop Demonizing Your 9–5

Everyone says, "Quit your 9–5 and chase your passion."

Here's the truth: If you don't come from money, quitting too soon will crush your passion before it even begins.

Passion doesn't run on inspiration. It runs on capital, time, and money. Bills don't disappear just because you've discovered your "calling." Without a stable income, you're not a full-time dreamer. You're a struggling actor, writer, or creator with a side of anxiety.

Your 9–5 is not your enemy. It's your training ground and launchpad.

The Hidden ROI of a 9–5

We've all been sold the story that a job is just a paycheck. But if you pay attention, your 9–5 is teaching you skills that will make or break you when you step into your own thing. Many demonize the 9–5 grind, and I refuse to side with them. Your job doesn't just pay the bills. It gives you the opportunity to build connections, be a great team player, and, most importantly, become a great leader.

It also teaches you:

- **Accountability:** You learn to deliver, not just start
- **Time management:** You can't "wing it" forever.
- **Communication:** You learn to pitch, present, and persuade.
- **Professionalism:** You show up on time, even when you don't feel like it.
- **Networking:** Your coworkers, clients, and bosses are potential allies.
- **Leadership:** You watch good and bad managers, and you learn from them.

Unburnable Ambition

The leadership and communication skills gained in regular jobs strongly predict future career success.[35] In other words: The office is your lab.

On an episode of *The Balance Theory* podcast, Tracy Harmoush said the corporate grind sucked the soul out of her. But she also admitted that she built a strong business only because of the discipline and ethics she learned in that very grind.[36]

Workplaces don't just pay bills. They develop learning and growth that support later entrepreneurial ventures.[37]

On an episode of *Rise & Tell*, I talked with Vivek N., a musician and tech leader.[38] His advice to aspiring creatives? Get your life in order first. A good-paying job funds your gear, your freedom, your art. He was upfront with his employer

---

[35] Peter Kuhn and Catherine Weinberger, "Leadership Skills and Wages," *Journal of Labor Economics* 23, no. 3 (2002).
[36] Tracy Harmoush, guest, *The Balance Theory*, season 6, episode 5, "Most People Get Motivation Completely Wrong | Tracy Harmoush," September 14, 2025.
[37] Toon W. Taris et al., "The Motivational Make-Up of Workaholism and Work Engagement: A Longitudinal Study on Need Satisfaction, Motivation, and Heavy Work Investment," *Frontiers in Psychology* 11 (2020).
[38] Vivek N., guest, *Rise & Tell with Sheekha*, episode 10, "How to Balance a Full Time Job and a Music Career with 23 Odd Cats," August 17, 2025.

about his music and built trust by always delivering on time. His lesson: Don't demonize your organization before you've even given them a chance to support you.

The pattern is clear: The 9–5 doesn't just pay your rent. It gives you the infrastructure to build a future.

So don't just demonize any culture until you've gotten a chance to learn something, because as an overachiever, you might find yourself on the other side of the fence one day, and you'll be judged for your leadership style and work ethic.

Tools to Use Your Job as a Launchpad

- **Audit your burnout:** Is it your job that's draining you, or poor boundaries, poor money habits, or the wrong role? Be honest.
- **Act like your future self:** Use weekends or PTO to test-drive your dream. Want to be a writer? Block one weekend as a writing retreat. See how it feels. (Spoiler: it might not be as romantic as you think.)
- **Leverage your benefits:** Health insurance, vacation days, even professional development budgets, these are assets. Use them.

- **Build your runway:** Save and stack cash from your job so that when you leap, you leap with a parachute, not a blindfold.
- **Mine your network:** The people you meet at work may be your first clients, investors, collaborators, or readers. Don't underestimate them.

The Real Truth

Stop treating your job as the villain. Stop glorifying the idea of burning bridges for passion. Your 9–5 is funding your dream, teaching you skills, and giving you a network you'd pay thousands for if you had to buy it.

The point isn't to stay in a job you hate forever. The point is to use it wisely while you build your exit.

Your job doesn't have to be your cage.

It can be your launchpad.

Chapter 12

Community and Connection

Burnout thrives in isolation.

One common thing among hustlers and overachievers irrespective of whether they are extroverts or introverts is that they struggle in isolation.

Ambitious people like us often think no one else will understand our goals or struggles, so we stay silent. We carry the weight alone. And in doing so, we let burnout win.

I used to believe asking for help meant I was weak. If I admitted I couldn't handle everything, people would finally say what I feared most: "You bit off more than you could chew."

The truth? Asking for help is not a weakness. It's a strategy.

The Cost of Doing It All Alone

When I realized video editing was draining me, I kept grinding anyway. I edited for hours on my walking pad one day and woke up with blisters on my feet. It took literal pain to admit what was obvious: I needed help.

I couldn't wear shoes, and it was the harshest winter Toronto had ever had in the last ten years.

Once I hired an editor, my burnout lifted almost overnight. I had a weekly system, better cadence, and more energy for what I actually loved: creating content. Paying someone didn't just save me time; it gave me accountability. If I was investing in help, I had to use it.

The same applied at home. I had to finally tell Simon, "I can't do it all. If I'm editing, I can't also cook"—we take turns cooking—"and manage chores." His response? "I got you. Focus on your content. I'll take care of the rest." That single conversation shifted our dynamic and lowered my stress more than any productivity hack.

Help was always available. I just had to ask.

Sometimes, you end up not seeing that you need help at your workplace too. We are hyperfixated and so deep in the task at hand that we forget to ask for help. Most of my team members fall into this habit, and as a leader, I have to remind them to share and ask for help whenever needed.

My favorite book, *Think and Get Rich* by Napoleon Hill, lists both traits of a good leader and causes of failure in leadership. The one that stuck with me was the habit of doing more than you're being paid for. Hill also mentions lack of imagination and fear of competition from followers as causes of failure. I remind myself and my teammates often that there's no need to overwork, especially when you have nine other teammates. Train someone else to be your backup. That way, you're not only avoiding burnout but also being a good leader.

Community as Prevention and Cure

Healthy relationships protect mental health.

Burnout doesn't just drain your body; it corrodes relationships. But community, whether a partner, a tribe of friends, or a professional network, acts as both prevention and cure.

Sheekha S.

As an immigrant, I found my tribe in cultural associations and local events. What started as a way to feel less homesick ended up becoming a safety net. These were the people who helped us move countries, shared my book release, checked in during tough times, and celebrated our milestones even from miles away.

That's the power of community: people who pull you out of the trench when you're sinking and hype you up when you're climbing.

The key is balance. Community should recharge you, not drain you. Recognize when social obligations tip into exhaustion, and practice saying no. A supportive community doesn't guilt you into burnout. It respects your boundaries.

Tools to Build Connection Without Burnout:

- **Support Map:** List your "go-to" people for different needs: emotional support, practical help, professional advice, etc.
- **Connection Ritual:** Pick one: a weekly walk with a friend, a Sunday call home, or a coffee chat. Consistency matters more than frequency.
- **Battery Check:** Write down two people who charge your energy and two who

drain it. Prioritize the chargers. Say no (politely) to the drainers.
- **Ask Practice:** Make one small request for help each week. It could be asking your partner to cook dinner, delegating a task at work, or hiring someone for a few hours. Practice receiving help as much as you practice giving it.

If you have kids, pets, and have multiple things that need your attention, start asking for help and actually take it.

It can get overwhelming really fast, and the only way you can start tackling burnout is by identifying these triggers and becoming self-aware.

Burnout isolates. Connection heals.

You don't need dozens of people, just a few who will tell you, "I got this. You rest."

Chapter 13

Designing Your Burnout-Proof Future

Consistency doesn't come from willpower. It comes from systems.

I learned this the hard way. For months, video editing and uploading content drained me until I finally hired an editor and content manager. Suddenly, my episodes had a rhythm, deadlines were met, and I felt lighter. Not because I was working harder but because I had a system that worked for me instead of against me.

That's when it clicked: Burnout isn't just about overworking. It's about operating without sustainable systems.

By the way, to those demonizing your 9–5, this is one of the skills that your daily job teaches you.

The Dangers of Decision Fatigue

Willpower is a finite resource. Every decision you make, no matter how small, chips away at it. This is called *decision fatigue* (or ego depletion). Over time, your ability to choose wisely deteriorates.[39]

Thus, if every single task depends on you figuring out what to do *in the moment*, you will exhaust yourself. Go easy and make efficient choices. Decisions shouldn't deplete your mental energy.

In 2023, Dutch researchers identified a reinforcing loop: *high workload → poor recovery → emotional exhaustion → less control → further overload.* They concluded that high workloads, work/life imbalance, and insufficient recovery time all exacerbate burnout.[40]

---

[39] Mona Maier et al., "Systematic Review of the Effects of Decision Fatigue in Healthcare Professionals on Medical Decision-Making," *Health Psychology Review* (2025): 1–46.

[40] Lisa S. Barsties et al., "A System Science Perspective on Burn-out: Development of an Expert-based Causal Loop Diagram," Frontiers in Public Health 11 (2023).

There are multiple books in the self-help genre that can teach you how to resolve issues with work-life balance. Several studies have examined decision fatigue and how to prevent it. Start with those resources now that you have identified what is causing you to burn out.

So far, we have outlined the thought and behavior patterns that overachievers struggle with and seen how we end up taking on more than we can handle. Now, we can talk about what helped me the most to correct those habits: building systems that I can follow consistently. Systems that could feed my mind and body and satiate the hunger of my ambitious personality.

Why Systems Matter

Building a process that works is crucial to any project, big or small. If you're someone who loves to stay organized and well informed on milestones and metrics, then you love systems.

Look around: Hospitals, airlines, software, even your morning coffee shop, they all run on systems. Without them, chaos takes over.

The same is true in our personal lives. Ambitious people think they can "power through" on passion alone. But passion without process leads straight to exhaustion.

In fact, research shows burnout is often rooted in system failures, not just personal weakness. Healthcare studies prove it: When structures collapse, individuals crumble.[41]

Burnout prevention isn't about doing less. It's about designing systems that protect your energy and priorities.

One of my favorite articles stated this:

> The cumulative effect of system failures can contribute to decreased morale and burnout of the workforce. While burnout manifests in individuals, it is fundamentally rooted in systems…Manifestations of burnout can be physical, such as exhaustion and insomnia, or psychological, including fatigue and decreased productivity. Burnout can also manifest in individuals emotionally, resulting in a lack of motivation, lack of empathy for patients, a sense of failure, disengagement, and a decreased sense of personal accomplishment.[42]

Toxic Self-Esteem

You know at every reunion, there's that one set of people who will point at the class toppers or bookworms and say something like, "Ah, wasn't she at the top of the class? What happened to

---

[41] Tait Shanafelt et al., "The Business Case for Investing in Physician Well-Being," *JAMA Internal Medicine* 177, no. 12 (1826–32).

[42] George Zangaro et al., "Impact of System Failures on Healthcare Workers," Agency for Healthcare Research and Quality, March 21, 2023.

her? What's she doing now? I thought she'd be a CEO one day."

Or

"Whatever happened to that bookworm? That backbencher is better than him. At least he ended up being a politician in his area."

I was that class topper who expected to become a CEO one day. Instead, I was running in circles, proving myself everywhere but moving nowhere. It wasn't due to lack of talent. The problem was I lacked systems.

On an episode of my podcast, Dr. Albert Bramante spoke about toxic self-esteem. He said, "With healthy self-esteem, you celebrate your achievements, your wins, and feel you're deserving. Now, toxic high self-esteem is when you take it to the point where you're better than everybody else."[43]

Most overachievers find themselves with this toxic self-esteem at least once in their lifetime. I used to think being a "one-woman show" meant I was strong. But running multiple projects

---

[43] Albert Bramante, guest, *Rise & Tell with Sheekha*, episode 41, "Stop Playing Small: Overcome Self-Doubt & Imposter Syndrome- Albert Bramante," October 13, 2025, 13 min., 13 sec.

without systems corroded me physically and emotionally.

When I finally built routines that matched my values, batching podcast tasks, using my calendar as a non-negotiable guide, and resetting quarterly, everything shifted. I wasn't just chasing goals. I was sustaining them.

Systems Create Freedom

When you design your life around sustainable processes, you protect the two things burnout steals first: your energy and your joy.

If you've come this far, you have not only learned some amazing tips to identify habits that are causing burnout but also some cool and effective frameworks to help manage it.

One last tool that has helped me immensely is to pause and look at others who aren't like you but are happy. It will be hard to reframe your mindset at first, but try to imagine a world where you have no overly ambitious goals, no big projects, and no deadlines. You'll find that you can still be happy and content all while finding purpose without burnout.

Scheduling

Being a high-performing employee doesn't mean your calendar should always be filled up with calls and meetings. Ever since I learned to design and map my ideal week, I feel lighter even when I have a *busy* day. I am a firm believer in managing my time and expectations, but don't let that affect your mental health.

Calendar clutter is still clutter.

There are multiple apps that can help you manage your calendars and track your habits. Schedule your time in a way that boosts your energy. Notice the feeling you get anytime you see a meeting on your calendar that doesn't make you happy.

Not all meetings are going to be productive, but notice which ones force you to fake a smile, and see if you can reschedule those in the future to a different time in the day or on a different day in the week. Time management isn't about squeezing in more meetings but about spacing them out correctly.

Researchers have recently begun studying "Zoom fatigue": how back-to-back meetings and lack of recovery and transition time can increase fatigue and burnout.[44]

One of my past clients always scheduled their meetings at five minutes after the hour: for

---

[44] Michele Webb, "Zoom Fatigue and How to Prevent It," *Journal of Registry Management* 48, no. 4 (2021): 181–182.

example, at 11:05 instead of 11:00 a.m. or 1:05 instead of 1:00 p.m. The idea was that by scheduling extra time in between back-to-back meetings, their employees could take a break and avoid being late to calls.

I also started to cancel meetings that could have been a Slack message or an email, and I declined meetings that I didn't need to attend. I noticed a significant difference in my energy at the end of the workday. I was ready to tackle my other tasks with a fair amount of battery left in me. I was happy to reschedule podcast recordings when I had cancelations from guests, and it didn't irk me even though I'd be fully prepped with my makeup done and light on.

I rewired my brain to be grateful for cancelations. I get to use that time to rest and reset. (Albeit a little overdressed, but, hey, who cares?)

When I audit my week, I make a mental note of whether I will be attending a certain call or not. I don't entertain random requests, and I protect my time. And my energy has never been better.

Tools to Build a System That Works for You

Here's the truth: Sustainable success is built, not stumbled into.

Unburnable Ambition

Your calendar should reflect your values, not just obligations. Your systems should serve your health, creativity, and joy, not just your hustle.

Tools:

- **Ideal Week Blueprint:** Map a week that balances work, rest, play, and growth. If your calendar has no white space, you don't have a system—you have a trap.
- **Burnout Firewall:** Identify early warning signs (like constant irritability or skipped meals). Create a "firewall" habit that stops the spiral—a walk, a boundary script, or a check-in with your support system.
- **Quarterly Reset:** Every three months, and review your goals, energy, and boundaries.

I personally love this system because I had a sticker on one of my monitors in June that said, "6 months left." I listed out my goals for the next two quarters, and I locked in.

One result of this exercise is this wonderful no-fluff book you're reading/listening to.

Chapter 14

Rising and Telling Your Story

Stories are how we rise. Stories are how we connect.

When Dr. Rod Berger joined me on *Rise & Tell*, our conversation wasn't just about media or journalism. It was about awareness. He said something that reshaped the way I think about storytelling: "If I'm not aware of my own potential biases, or the perceived bias I may be bringing into an environment, then I'm doing a disservice. Because that means I'm thinking more about me than I am about the individual and their story."[45]

That hit hard. Because storytelling isn't just about words. It's about presence. It's about stepping into someone else's world with humility, not authority. Culture plays a massive role in how stories are told and understood. Rod talked about being the only white face for miles in some places and realizing that awareness, not assumption, was the bridge.

That's what *Rise & Tell* was always meant to be. It wasn't a platform for noise but a space for nuance. For connection across continents, accents, and lived realities.

Storytelling is not about us. It's about what happens through us. The exchange, the empathy, and the understanding that bridges worlds. That's the power of storytelling. It turns struggle into survival guides. It transforms burnout into wisdom others can lean on.

Why Your Story Matters

We grow up on stories, bedtime tales, cultural myths, family histories. But as adults, we forget that our lived experiences are also stories. And they are often the ones people need most.

---

[45] Rod Berger, unpublished episode, 46 min., 23 sec.

I want you to own your story, no matter where you come from or where you live right now. Stories are what make you interesting. But your story needs to tell the truth. No fake filters.

When I started sharing my own burnout journey, I wasn't sure anyone cared. But the messages I received proved otherwise: "This is exactly what I'm going through." "I thought I was alone."

Here's the truth: Your story doesn't have to be polished. It just has to be real. The world doesn't need another polished highlight reel. It needs your unfiltered humanity.

Break the Stigma

We often hear about burnout from global names like Mel Robbins or Jay Shetty. But the immigrant narrative? Cultural guilt? The pressure of leaving home with two suitcases, a student visa, and the silent weight of everyone's expectations riding on your shoulders? That story is missing.

Where is the story about the immigrant son working three jobs while pretending on video calls that everything is fine?

Where is the story of the girl who was promised a luxurious, golden life abroad, a fairytale marriage, a house, and a future but now finds herself on a dependent visa, navigating job applications, loans, babies, bills, and the crushing loneliness of a life that was supposed to be easier?

Where is the story about the boy who worked overtime for months to pay for his father's surgery and missed a call informing him of his father's death?

Where is the story of the man who couldn't go home to see his daughter being born because being an immigrant is never as simple and easy as buying a ticket home?

And what about the families who arrived in new countries with hope stitched into their passports, only to be met with high taxes, endless paperwork, and the cruel irony of opportunity they can't fully access? They dream of calling this new place home, but they can't because rest is never taught, and success has always been measured incorrectly.

These are the stories we don't hear on the top podcasts or see in the glossy bestselling self-help books. But they're real. They're raw. And they matter. And that's why we need more of us to rise and tell our truths.

Power of Owning Your Narrative

Your story is the one thing no algorithm can replicate. No one else has lived your version of success, loss, burnout, or recovery. That uniqueness is your superpower.

Sharing your story doesn't just help others; it heals you. Brené Brown's research shows vulnerability builds connection and breaks shame. The moment you speak it out loud, you take back power. Your story could be someone else's survival guide. Sharing your burnout journey breaks stigma.

We've been told that our value lies in our productivity. But storytelling reminds us that our value lies in our perspective. Owning your narrative is part of healing. It's also part of leadership.

When you rise and tell your story, you're showing others what resilience actually looks like, not the motivational-poster kind, but the kind with dark circles under its eyes and hope in its heart.

Stop glorifying toxic hustle.

Here are a few things I did that helped me.

Tools to Share Your Story

Story Starter

Break your journey into three acts:

- **Before:** What life looked like before burnout.
- **During:** The crash, the signs, the struggles.
- **After:** How you're recovering, and what you're learning.

I once joined a workshop called Working Title with Hollywood producer Capella Fahoome, where she guided us to view our lives through the lens of filmmaking. Our first step was to map our life into a three-act structure. That exercise was uncomfortable, raw, and transformative. I highly recommend you try it.

Impact Map

Ask yourself: Who could this story help right now? A coworker? A fellow immigrant? A younger version of yourself? Share it with them—even privately.

I created a journal, "30 Days to Recover from Burnout."

Healing isn't all soft lights and meditation apps. Sometimes it feels like pulling out a stubborn hair stuck in your ass crack during a shower, annoying, messy, and unavoidable. But once you deal with it, relief comes.

That's the spirit I want you to carry: honest, messy, imperfect progress.

I still want you to identify as an overachiever and a highly ambitious person but one that's not going through burnout.

Your Mondays Are Limited

Jodi Wellman's book *You Only Die Once* reminds us that the average person has about four thousand Mondays.[46] That number hit me hard.

Four thousand chances to reset.

Four thousand opportunities to choose meaning over maintenance.

Ask yourself: Do you want the rest of your Mondays to be drained, exhausted, and numb? Or do you want them to matter to you, not just to the world watching?

Because the truth is ambition without alignment is burnout wearing lipstick.

---

[46] Jody Wellman, *You Only Die Once* (Voracious, 2024).

Rise & Tell

Your story is not a weakness. It's your proof of resilience. When you share it, you give others permission to rise too. You've walked through the fire, and now you carry the light.

This isn't just the end of a book. It's the beginning of a conversation. One where you get to redefine success, reclaim your voice, and rebuild your fire on your own terms.

And if you've listened to my podcast, you know how I end every episode. Because it applies here as well, maybe more than anywhere else:

Keep Growing.

Keep Glowing.

And Be Yourself.

This is your host, Sheekha Singh, signing off.

But your story?

It's just beginning.

THE END

Afterword

If you made it here, THANK YOU! And Congratulations!

You proved that your attention span is more than the average person's seven seconds. If you've redefined success on your own terms after reading this and no longer chase the definition that was handed to you, then I've done my job and will consider this book a success.

Burnout is not a new topic, and this certainly isn't the first book on burnout ever published, but it's the first one from an immigrant's point of view. I decided on this topic after a lot of brainstorming and wrote the book after thorough research. I saw a gap on bookstore shelves, and I wanted to fill that space with an immigrant's voice. One that is fresh, raw, and personal.

Sheekha S.

Whether you're an overachiever or not, whether you're ambitious or not, my hope is to generate enough awareness on burnout and how it creeps up. I wanted to generate buzz around how culture plays a major role in careers, decisions, and to-do lists, especially in this day and age.

I sincerely hope this book inspires you to pause and realize what success means to you, and I hope this time it includes a well-rested version of you. I hope you realize that you are not alone in a world that is obsessed with automations and optimizations. I wish you all the best, and I hope your ambitions are unburnable from this moment forward.

Acknowledgments

Thank you to everyone who tuned in to my podcast, *Rise & Tell*. You inspire me to do more, dream louder, and speak my truth even when it's messy.

A huge thank you to my editor, Samantha Hendrix, for turning my chaos into clarity and most of all for being honest!

To all the ARC readers who took time out of their already full lives to read, highlight, and send thoughtful reviews. Truly grateful.

To Simon, my forever devil's advocate, first beta reader, and the only person who can handle my half-assed drafts without judgment. (Okay, maybe some judgment...okay, maybe a lot!) I owe you a lot more beers and biryani. Thanks for always keeping me humble.

Sheekha S.

To my mom and sister, for being my biggest cheer leaders all across the world, and to Onyx, for sitting beside me through every late-night writing/editing session.

And finally, to my video editor and content manager, Muhammad Tayyab. You've made my life easier.

Thank you all for being the reason *Unburnable Ambition* became more than just a manuscript. It became my reminder that accountability and love are what truly keep the fire burning.

About the Author

Sheekha Singh is an author, podcaster, and unapologetic over-achiever learning to redefine success without burnout. Born and raised in India and now living in Canada, she brings a unique perspective shaped by cultural expectations, immigrant grit, and a decade-long career in tech leadership.

Sheekha is the host of *Rise & Tell with Sheekha*, a podcast featuring conversations with entrepreneurs, creatives, and leaders about growth, resilience, and telling the stories that matter. She also runs multiple travel and lifestyle YouTube channels while writing both nonfiction and fiction—including her upcoming sci-fi romance.

With over eleven years of experience as a QA leader, Scrum Master, a certified Product Owner, and speaker, Sheekha blends personal narrative with practical tools to help ambitious professionals escape toxic hustle, reclaim their energy, and build lives that feel as good on the inside as they look on paper.

When she isn't writing or recording, you can find her traveling, sipping a craft beer, or chasing sunsets with her husband and their dog, Onyx.

Rise. Tell. Rest. Repeat. That's her mantra and the heartbeat of everything she creates.

Connect With Me

Love this book? Don't forget to leave a review! Every review matters, and it matters a *lot* to me! Head over to Amazon or wherever you purchased this book to leave an honest review for me.

I thank you endlessly.

For exciting updates, join our mailing list: www.sheekhasingh.com/unburnable-ambition

Also, don't forget to post a picture on social media with the hashtags #riseandtellwithsheekha and #unburnableambition. Tag me in your pictures! I love them, and they make my day!

You can also get a copy of my 30-day free burnout recovery journal! Email me for more details: riseandtellwithsheekha@gmail.com

www.ingramcontent.com/pod-product-compliance
Lightning Source LLC
Chambersburg PA
CBHW060400080526
44583CB00012B/400